The Flower

Chris Baines
& Penny Ives

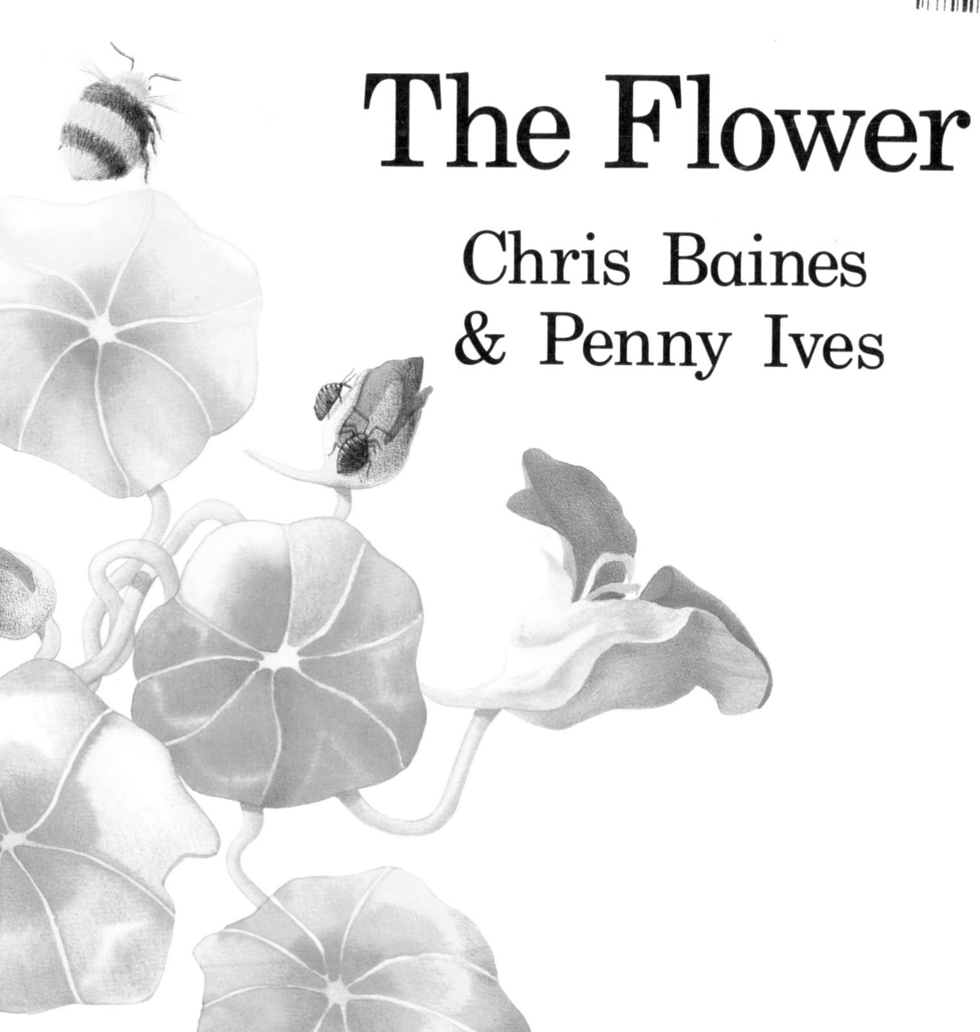

FRANCES LINCOLN
WINDWARD

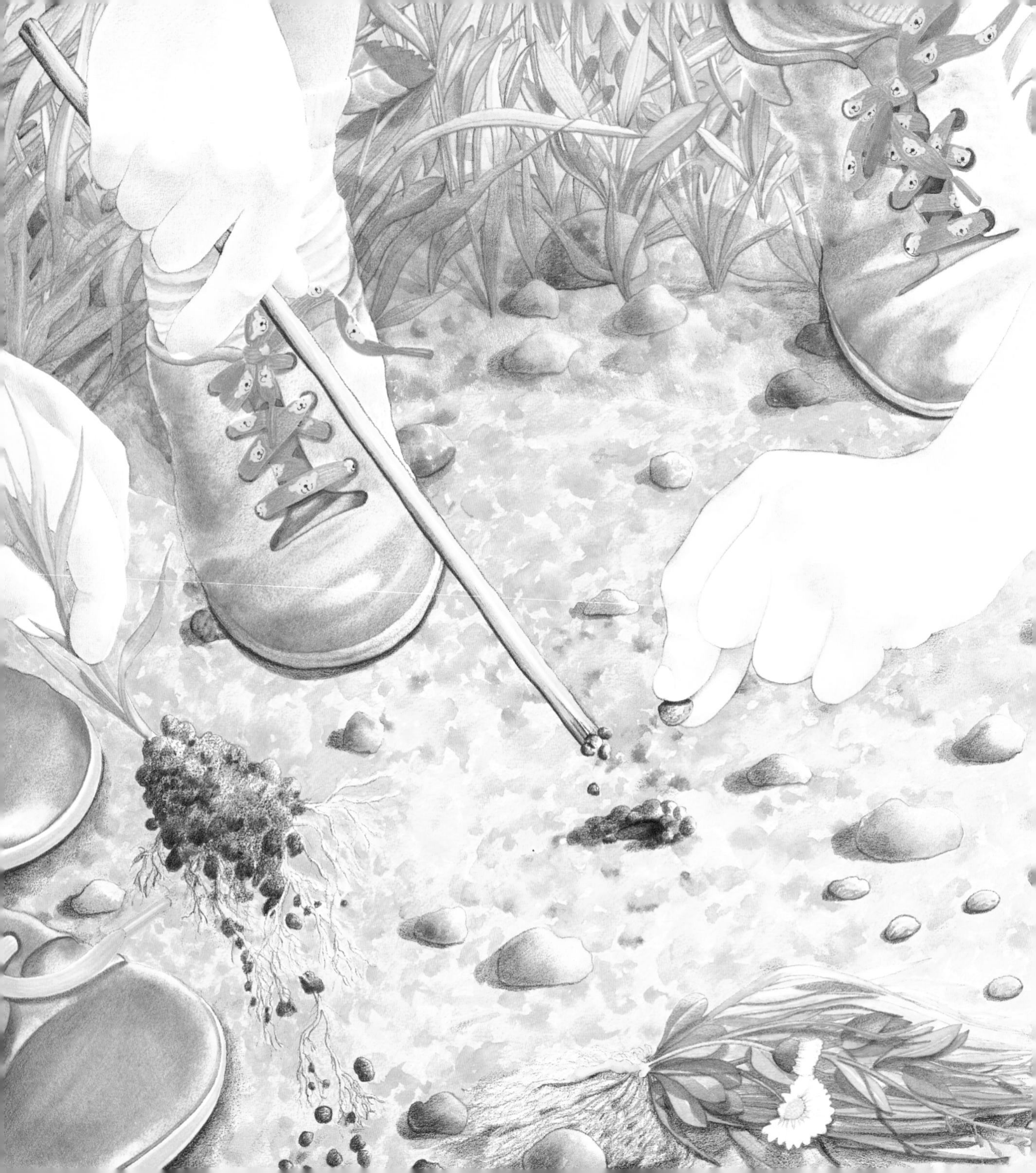

The children have saved up some money, and they buy a packet of seeds. There's a lovely picture on the packet, but can those little brown seeds really turn into such a pretty plant? The children make a garden. They plant one of the little brown seeds and water it every day.

At first nothing seems to be happening – but it is! Down in the dark damp earth the seed swells and bursts. A fat shoot grows up through the earth, and two round green leaves open in the sunshine. At the same time, a thin white root is growing down, deep into the earth. It soaks up water to make the new plant grow. The new plant needs lots of water and lots of sunshine. When weeds start to grow, the children pull them out to give their plant plenty of room.

But the plant is being nibbled by something. Every night, when the children are in bed, some hungry snails slide into their garden and nibble holes in the leaves of the new plant. The snails always disappear back to their holes before the sun comes up, but they leave behind shiny, silvery trails. The children wonder what can be making the silvery patterns on the leaves.

They watch their new plant very carefully, and discover all kinds of tiny animals living on it. Little black bugs are sucking juicy sap out of the stems. Now a bright red ladybird gobbles up some of the bugs. There are lots of ants running up and down the plant too. They chase the ladybird away, and as a reward they collect some sweet sticky juice from the bugs and carry it back to their nest.
Early one wet shiny morning the children see a snail. It has made a silver trail – and the trail leads back to the plant. Now they know who the secret leaf nibblers are!
The children like snails. They are happy to share their garden with all the little animals that live there.

At last the first pretty flower is open. A big bee crawls inside and sucks up the sweet, sugary nectar. When the bee buzzes off to the next flower, it is covered all over in yellow, powdery pollen. The flower and the bee make the children happy, but some of the leaves and shoots on their new plant are twisted and sad. It's all those little animals. They seem to be spoiling it.

The children ask a grown-up for help. “Those little black bugs are pests,” he tells them. “Keep away while I kill them for you with my poison spray.” Pssst! In no time at all he sprays the plant with poison.

After it's been sprayed the plant looks happier, but nearly all the tiny animals are dead. There are just one or two clever bugs hiding under a leaf.

The plant grows very fast now, and so do the bugs. Soon there are lots of new baby bugs too. Help! The children don't want anyone to spray more poison, but they do want to save their plant.
What can they do?

Suddenly they remember the
bright red ladybird who gobbled
up bugs. This gives them an idea.

The children search among the wild plants
that grow around their little garden.
What can they be looking for?